Without Majesty

A Reflection on the Last Words
of Jesus, the Christ

Sylvia Dains

Without Majesty: A Reflection on the Last Words of Jesus, the Christ
ISBN: Softcover 978-1-946478-47-4
Copyright © 2017 by Sylvia Dains

All rights reserved. No part of this book may be reproduced or transmitted in any form or by any means, electronic or mechanical, including photocopying, recording, or by any information storage and retrieval system, without permission in writing from the publisher.

Parson's Porch Books is an imprint of **Parson's Porch & Book Publishers** in Cleveland, Tennessee, which has double focus. We focus on the needs of creative writers who need a professional publisher to get their work to market, **&** we also focus on the needs of others by sharing our profits with those who struggle in poverty to meet their basic needs of food, clothing, shelter and safety.

Without Majesty

Contents

Foreword 5

Prologue 11

1 Forgiveness 21

2 Thief 23

3 Pieta 29

4 Jesus 36

5 I'm thirsty 40

6 Mission Accomplished 43

7 Surrender 48

About the Author 53

Acknowledgements 55

Foreword

Thank you for opening this book. It represents a journey long in its wandering: from certainty to doubt, from confidence to questioning, from searching to discovery. When it was darkest, I remembered some long-ago voice telling the child I was to join my sufferings to those of Jesus. It wasn't until all of the easier, more comfortable alternatives had been tried and found lacking that I finally found the courage to climb up onto the cross, out of the dark night. There I found welcome, struggle, and, ultimately, peace.

This is an unusual rendering of the Seven Last Words in that it concentrates more on the humanity of Jesus: in his use of contemporary language, in his expressions of anguish as he begs the Father's mercy, in his triumph over his own human doubting and his final letting go in full trust, turning over his spirit to the infinite Mercy he always knew awaited him. My rationale comes from the Eucharistic prayer that describes him as "one like us in all things but sin". I took that to imply that even Jesus -- God though he was -- could be subject to uncertainty at times, to hurt feelings when friends disappointed him, to times of impatience, anger, loss, frustration and ambivalence.

And so, I dedicate this effort to all who take the time to reflect on the mystery of deep love that God holds out to each of us; and who accept the call to share it and the challenge to live it.

Sylvia Dains

Without beauty, without majesty, we saw him: a man of sorrows, familiar with pain... and we took no account of him ...[1]

---

[1]from "With what great Love," ©1976 by Carey Landry. Published by OCP Publications, Portland, OR, www.ocp.org from the recording "All is Well with my Soul" and "Abba! Father!" Used with permission.

Prologue

Jerusalem

It's Passover time! The streets are especially busy today, with people making their last-minute preparations for the Great Feast. There is an air of festival as they hurry about, greeting one another and exchanging pleasantries. The whole scene is charged with the joy of reuniting friends and family members coming from faraway places, bringing stories, small keepsakes, and treats for the children. It's noisy, happy confusion as friend discovers friend and they welcome one another joyfully.

Perhaps the happiest of all are the street vendors, because this time of year, with its excitement and spirit of celebration, offers the hope and possibility of brisk sales and healthy profits.

Suddenly there's a change: voices become louder, more excited, and attention shifts toward the city gate. We turn to investigate the source of the clamor just in time to see a young man astride a donkey enter through the gate, and we join the crowd in enthusiastic welcome. The roar has exploded into a thundering celebration as people remove their cloaks and place them in his path. Some are waving palm branches, and a chorus of "Hosanna!" fills the air.

It is good to be here!

Gethsemane

Jesus and his friends enter the Garden of Olives, not far from the place where they have just shared the Passover meal. Jesus is pensive and after a short time, takes Peter, James and John with him, apart from the others. Now he seems troubled, asks the three to "Watch and pray", walks a few steps away from them, and falls into deep prayer as his friends are overcome by sleep.

> Father
> so often have I come to you
> to ask for strength
> for courage for the work
> and you have never failed me
> never left me.
>
> But tonight my courage fails me.
> I beg you: take this cup from me.
>
> The wine is bitter
> with the taste of failure.
> My voice cries out to you --
> comes back to me in melancholy echo.
> Where is your comfort, Father?
> Where the hand on my shoulder
> steadying and strengthening?

> Tonight I walk in faith.
> I beg you: if you will,
> take from me this cup;
> but not my will, Father.
> May your will be done in me.
>
> If this cup in truth is mine
> I will take it in my hands.
> With thanks I will hold it to my heart
> > and bless
> > and drink.

During the course of his prayer, Jesus has stopped three times to wake the others and again ask them to pray -- but to no avail. It's been an emotional night; they may have over-indulged a bit, and sleep has continued to claim them.

Jesus and his companions are leaving the garden just as Judas approaches, accompanied by armed soldiers and Jewish guards. With a kiss, Judas sets in motion the events of the rest of the night. Jesus is arrested, bound, and taken before the high priest. During the ensuing questioning, accusations, and beatings, Jesus refuses to be intimidated,

Without Majesty

standing firmly in his truth and silently challenging the authority of the questioners.

Suddenly, it seems, the crowd, so overjoyed to welcome him just a few days ago, has become an angry mob, participating in a nightmare.

Why???!!

The Crowd

We've heard all we need to know! We watched the imposter get away with overturning the temple tables, working on the Sabbath, and defying the authority of the elders and the Pharisees. He violated Torah, and claimed to have brought a "new" commandment.

We saw him before the governor. He had a chance to admit to the charge of blasphemy; but instead he declared himself a king, saying that his kingdom is "not of this world".

From where, then?

And so we freed Barabbas.

When Pilate asked what should happen to this man, we all shouted with one voice:

"Crucify him!"

We see now before us the result of that demand. It's his own fault, really; all he would have had to do was answer the governor's questions -- show some respect for authority.

Instead, he has become a reminder to all who would scorn the law.

We can stay only a little while longer to enjoy the spectacle. Then we must hurry home -- so much to do to prepare the feast that celebrates our deliverance from persecution and injustice.

Judas

Judas stands on a rocky height overlooking the town, remembering and regretting the evening's events and the role he embraced for the sake of money. The impact, the meaning of his act, is so much more cruel than he had imagined -- and now the crowd is calling for Jesus' death!

He ponders:
It never occurred to me that the priests, those men who hold themselves up as examples before the people, had in mind what I've seen tonight.

Looking down from here, I can see what has been unfolding. I've seen them whip him, beat him when he fell, prod him like some beast of burden. I can hear them, can envision their faces as they call for his blood. The only voice I haven't heard has been his own: defending his innocence, protesting their cruelty, begging for mercy.

To think that I have brought this about!
To think that I have sunk this low!

> Tonight in the garden
> I kissed him
> and the soldiers came.
> So simple
> but I hadn't bargained for
> the disappointment in his eyes
> loving me
> convicting and forgiving me
> and as they seized him
> dragged him away like any criminal--
> I heard him call me "friend".

Golgotha

The cross is taken from Jesus' shoulder and placed on the ground, and he is ordered to lie down on it. From among the soldiers, one is chosen and handed the hammer and a large spike. He kneels, places the nail into Jesus' wrist joint, and raises the hammer. In that instant, his eyes catch a quick look at Jesus' face. He stops, hammer suspended, and their eyes meet. It's only a moment; but in that moment, the soldier sees Jesus looking back at him with love. In that moment, he falters; but then he remembers that "an order is an order"; and he brings down the hammer with full force. All that can be heard is the crack of the hammer hitting the nail, and Jesus' cry of pain.

> The last thing I wanted to do
> was be the one
> to nail him to the cross.
> But -- an order is an order.
> There is a heavy penalty
> for insubordination.
> In the execution of that order,
> I saw his eyes forgiving me,
> and forever
> I will grieve my part in it.

1

Forgiveness

It's getting late. The sky is overcast. Jesus, close to death, is in and out of consciousness, his breathing shallow and labored. Looking down from the cross, he can see dimly through the haze of blood and sweat dripping into his eyes. Everything is a blur; but he can discern that people have begun to leave. Soldiers are drawing lots for his tunic as normal activity slowly returns.

To give his arms some relief and offer a slight change of position, Jesus must steady his feet against the block under them and raise his body -- an excruciating act. But it is the price of each breath.

Since the beginning of this torment last night, Jesus has remained mostly silent; but now he wants to speak. He struggles for a breath and gathers as much strength as he can. Through the power of the Spirit, his voice comes forth, clear and loud enough to be heard....

> --in the street...
> --in the temple...
> --in the courtyard...

--in the garden...
--on the heights...

--by the crowd who cried for his death...
--by the soldier who wielded the hammer...
--by the schemers: the scribes, the Pharisees, and the high priests...
--by Pilate, who abandoned him to the mob...
--by Peter, who denied him...
--by Judas, who betrayed him...
--by each of us and for all generations......

Father, forgive them;
they don't know what they are doing.

2

Thief

Look at him! We were both arrested last night and shared a cell on death row. When I first saw him, he was covered with blood and spittle, his back torn to shreds by the whips. He said very little -- and in that place of shrieking and cursing and agony, **his silence** was the loudest thing I heard. Blasphemy, they said. I can hardly imagine him guilty of *any* charge -- but **blasphemy?**

Early today, the three of us were taken from our cells to be brought here. The other thief and I found our crosses already in place; but this man was made to carry his cross on his shoulders the whole distance from the prison, staggering under its weight as he made his way slowly and painfully up the hill. I saw him fall three times, and watched as **no one** helped him get up. In fact, with each fall he was beaten even more savagely, if that were possible.

Eventually someone was pulled from the crowd and forced to carry the cross for a short distance. And once I saw a woman push her way through the angry crush, remove her veil, and use it to wipe the blood and sweat from his face. Other than that, he has struggled alone, burdened with the weight he carries and accompanied by the taunts of the mob and the soldiers' repeated, relentless blows to his body.

His mother and his friends have followed along, not far behind. Their faces reveal their grief and anguish at seeing him treated like this and knowing they can't do anything to stop it. I winced each time he fell, and wished that **someone** would find the compassion to help him. All I could do was watch; it took my attention away from myself and my pain. I wondered: what kind of man is this: What could he have done to provoke this much anger and hate?

Who is this man? All I know about him I 've learned from gossip -- tales about bringing someone back from the dead, healing blind and lame people, and feeding a crowd of

5000. I've heard that children love to hear his stories about what heaven is like: stories about a wedding feast, a farmer planting seeds, a runaway son. What was there in any of that to incite the violence I'm seeing today?

The story of that rebellious son stays with me now. I remember growing up in the ghetto -- an angry, rebellious kid mired in poverty, but full of big dreams of wealth and privilege. I became a master at the art of relieving people of their valuables and evading authority. There was something addictive about getting away with it. How I loved making a mockery of the law! But I got a little too convinced of my own resourcefulness, and was arrogant enough to believe that I was smarter than the rest of them, that my life-style would never catch up with me.

Life has proven me wrong.

Now I hang on a cross I built with my life, next to an angry, belligerent thief and this quiet, gentle man who is being killed -- for **blasphemy??**

It strikes me that this is the first time in my life I have ever felt concern for another human. This man Jesus, without saying one word, has awakened in me feelings of concern, of compassion, of remorse. My concentration has shifted from my own pain and become empathy for his. At least, **I** am guilty; what has *he* done to deserve the treatment he has endured today -- the death sentence imposed on him?

From here I can see him clearly: eyes half closed and pain written all over his face. As his body sags under its own weight, the nails in his hands and feet tear at his flesh. A crown of thorns forced into his scalp has matted his hair and bloodied his face. Altogether, this man is the most broken, defeated figure I've ever seen. And yet -- I heard him speak a few minutes ago, asking God to forgive the crowd that is still shouting, demanding that he prove that he is the Son of God by coming down from the cross.

Forgive??!!!

Forgive???!!!

I can't believe that **no one** is defending this innocent man. One by one, his friends have begun to leave. Standing close are his mother, leaning on a young man, and a few other women.

My strength is fading; I can't live much longer. I am aware of a need to speak to him, an urgent sense of "now or never". I struggle to turn my head, to look at him one more time. The other thief has joined the crowd, insulting Jesus and demanding that he come down from the cross if he wants people to believe in him; and I've had enough: enough yelling, enough insults, enough of all of this.

With what is left of my strength, I shout:

"Have you no fear of God? After all, we are getting what we deserve!"

Jesus looks at me. Even in his agony, his look is penetrating. His eyes pierce past my face, to my very heart. I am caught up in his gaze. He *sees* me -- just as I am:

>--all I have been, and failed to become
>--all I have done, and failed to do

but his look is love, unconditional, as I have never experienced love.

In this moment, nothing else exists except the two of us. I can no longer hear the shouts or see the angry faces. All I can see are those eyes, loving me and drawing me into their unspoken blessing. My heart is moved, and I am startled by the sound of my own voice, praying:

"Jesus, remember me when you come into your kingdom."

Fear grips me as I come back to myself and remember who I am. Why should he bother with me? --and then, as I breathe my last breath, I hear him speak, and I am lifted by his words:

"I say to you: this day -- this very day -- you will be with me in paradise."

3

Pieta

> Standing with the women
> she watches his approach
> hardly recognizing
> the bloody, wounded body
> of her son.
> At the sight of him
> she gasps,
> and the tears begin--
> free and unrestrained.
>
> Strong arms hold her up,
> keep her from collapse.
> But then
> she squares her shoulders
> lifts her head boldly
> and follows unwaveringly
> behind the Victim
> to the place of final Yielding.

Standing here looking up at my son, I'm remembering the day Joseph and I presented him in the temple. It was a proud moment for us as Simeon took him into his arms and praised God for his birth. But then he said to me the words that have haunted me until this moment:

"A sword will pierce your very soul, that the thoughts of many hearts may be revealed."

I didn't understand it then; but as I stand here now, I can feel my heart breaking.

I think back to the night he was born in the cave at Bethlehem as heaven and earth rejoiced to welcome him. I remember his perfect little body: fragile and sturdy, helpless and powerful all at once. I treasure the memory of precious times when I held him in my arms and sang him to sleep, brushing back the curls from his beautiful face, and wondering what his future would be.

Today, I know.

I watched him grow and experience childhood's joys and hurts, triumphs and disappointments. I felt every skinned knee and bruise, every rejection. Every time he cried, I wanted to take him in my arms and love the hurt away. But I had to learn, as all mothers do, that we can't protect our children from life, with its pain, its injustices, its cruelty. All we can do is stand close and feel their pain with them, offering whatever comfort and encouragement we can. But I could never have guessed that violence could take such proportions as I have seen today; or that his life journey would lead here.

But -- today, I know.

I remember losing him on the way home from Jerusalem when he was twelve. Joseph and I each thought he was with the other. We searched frantically for three days, retracing our steps, asking relatives and friends; but **no one** had seen him. We were beside ourselves with worry. It was such a relief to finally find him -- in the temple --teaching the elders with the words: "Today this prophecy is fulfilled in your hearing." I chided him, asking, "Why have you done this? Didn't you know that we would worry?" His response: "Don't **you** know that I must be about my Father's work?" -- brought me to the sudden realization that his was a mission unlike any other. But who could have known that **this** would be the place of final fulfillment?
Today, all of us know.

My son grew to manhood and became a teacher, a healer, a compassionate friend to the friendless, never turning anyone away. He lived every moment of his life in service to the will of his Father in heaven. Crowds followed him, children loved him; and he offered life and hope to everyone. His stories gave insights into the great love God holds out to all of us. Now he hangs on a cross, a victim of his own call; and gladly would I change places with him.

I search the face of the suffering man on the cross, looking for any trace of the little boy I remember. Can this be the same person? But I have been here since the beginning, and I cannot deny that this wounded, battered man is my child. His face, so beautiful and compassionate, is contorted with pain, covered with blood. His eyes, always so full of fire, excitement, and conviction, are dull and have lost all expression. Seeing him like this is unbearable, yet I can't turn my eyes away from him.

Without Majesty

I remember his words: always inviting and consoling, always healing the suffering and accepting the sinner -- but rebuking injustice and hypocrisy wherever he encountered them.

> "Your sins are forgiven."
> "Come to me...I will give you rest."
> "Stand up...walk!"
> "The Father and I are one."
> "Let the one without sin cast the first stone."
> "...you have made my house a den of thieves!"

Was it his **words** that finally became the sword they used against him?

Whenever he spoke, people listened; and the **way** he spoke did two things; it gave life, and got him into trouble. He was recognized as a prophet, and knew that a prophet could not be appreciated at home. So my son walked right into this, aware of the risks. He realized this could not end well; but he also knew that he had to be true to his call. And now he hangs on a cross: humiliated, degraded, abandoned by those he called "friend" -- the very ones he chose, the ones he loved.

Where are they now?

People have been leaving, going home to prepare for Passover. Peter and the others have long since left. Only John and I remain, along with a few of the women, standing at the foot of the cross -- at the feet of the Victim: **standing our ground** against the hate and the hurt, the prejudice and violence of the world: because **this is where we must be.**

Through his trial and his torture and as he carried his cross, he was silent. He who in life was voice for the voiceless, became the victim, mute before the abuse and degradation -- speaking no word to defend himself. Now from the cross he has broken his silence to speak absolution to his murderers, deliverance to a thief, submission to the Father.

Once again, Simeon and his prophecy come to mind. Indeed, today my heart is pierced -- no, shattered -- as I watch my child losing his

Without Majesty

hold on life and recognize my helplessness before the reality of it.

For the rest of my life, I will bear the pain of this loss.

For the rest of my life, I will carry the image of his face, his body, so twisted and broken.

For the rest of my life, I will remember Jesus, my baby boy, providing for me.

Even in his agony, he still takes care of us.

"John....please.... take my mother home."

4

Jesus

I am so tired. My whole body screams with pain, and to breathe I must brace my feet against the block of wood beneath them and raise my body as much as I can. It takes all the strength I have; the pain is excruciating and the effort is exhausting. The thieves on either side of me have died, and their suffering is over. The crowd is thinning as people go their separate ways. Peter has left, in tears. Judas is gone as well. Where are the others -- those who said only last night that they could drink from the cup I was offering? Only John remains, with my mother and the other women, keeping vigil.

Father, what did I do wrong? All of my life was spent in obedience to your will for me. At my baptism in the Jordan, I heard your voice say to those gathered:

"This is my beloved son, in whom I am well pleased; listen to him." Later, on the Mount of Tabor, you said it again, and again you admonished people to listen. And some did. I remember telling them how blessed they are when they are slandered and rejected. But today, I have been slandered and rejected; and I do not feel blessed. I feel so alone. I feel like a failure. I know *you* have not failed, Father; but I wonder whether I could have somehow misunderstood the mission you gave me. Did I care too much about the Pharisees and the chief priests? Should I have approached them differently? If I had acted differently, would Peter have denied me, or Judas sold me like a slave? Would James and John and the others still be here with me instead of running away?

You are silent, Father, and I am so lonely. I think about times of celebration with my friends -- laughing with the children -- the good I was able to do through the power of our Spirit -- and I am thankful for all of that. But, even though I knew where my destiny would lead me, is it possible that, deep down,

I told myself that you would never let me come to such an end? Father, did I forget who I was and fall too much in love with my humanity? Did I become *too* human? What could I have done differently?

It's getting dark, and the pain and throbbing are constant and unrelenting. I no longer hear the jeers of the crowd nor the insults of the guards. I no longer hear the voice of Peter disowning me or the sound of the whip, striking and tearing my flesh. I hear the laughter of the soldiers as they roll dice to see who will go home with my tunic. My mother wove that tunic for me, and its only value comes from the fact that it came from her hands. If any one of these soldiers had asked me for it, I would have given it gladly. Why, then, does it offend me to see it become the trophy in a game of chance? Above the noise of the storm in my head, I can hear the soft weeping of the women looking up at me.

How long, Lord? How long must it be before I can come home? What else can I do to bring your kingdom to this people? Is there still something I have left undone? Is it too late? Father, I beg you: let me see your face; surround me with your love.

Have I not yet done enough? Father, I am hungry to hear your voice; I beg you to comfort me, because I feel -- forsaken.

> **Abba -- Father--**
> **why have you abandoned me?**

5

I'm thirsty.

Is there no one to give me a drink?

Since my arrest last night, I have endured assault and violation at the hands of a people I thought I knew, but no longer recognize. I have lost a great amount of blood, and have been offered neither water nor food since my arrest -- not even the compassion of a single drop of water. My mouth is so dry, my lips so parched, that I can barely generate even the smallest amount of saliva. Even my teeth are dry, and *not one* person has come with so much as a drop of water to give me the slightest bit of relief. The thirst is unbearable.

But there is another thirst at work here as well, a deeper thirst: I came to my mission thirsty for souls -- for hearts refreshed by love. My friends and I worked day and night for the sake of that thirst, a thirst that is unquenchable as long as there is still one lost

Without Majesty

sheep looking for home. It was for that thirst that I was bold in the face of authority -- merciful to the sinner -- compassionate to the grieving. It was for *their* thirst that I thirsted. Some did come; but others found me too much for them, and went away, still thirsty. It is for those that I thirst today. To them I say: "Come to the water! All you who thirst, who have nothing, come! Bring your children and your elders; bless each other with this water and drink your fill! And then, give each other a drink!"

My people: when you do this, my thirst **will** be less. It is when you recognize in each other that same yearning, and offer the cup in my name, that you minister to my thirst. Don't hold back; the more you are willing to hold the cup for the other to drink, the less you will be thirsty.

I see someone approach with a sponge on the end of a long stick. Holding it up, he offers it. As I taste, I recognize that it is vinegar; so I refuse it. The acidity has been enough to worsen, if that is possible, the dryness of my mouth. All I feel is the disappointment of a desire unquenched, a craving unsatisfied.

I beg you, all of you here with me: understand the depth of thirst in the world. Hear the cries of their yearning, and recognize my voice.

I stand at the well, holding out to you the living water that is my love for you: deep, endless, life-giving. You have only to reach out your hand and accept it; and then hold the cup for the other to drink.

Can you do this?

Will you do this?

It will never be too late; as long as there is one of you left still willing, you will be ministering to my thirst.

It's up to you.

My people – I'm still thirsty.

6

Mission Accomplished.
Father, the work you gave me to do, I have done.

I look down from here and see that only a few remain. It breaks my heart to see the pain in my mother's eyes. I know that John will take good care of her, and that gives me peace.

But I wonder: What went so wrong?

I worshipped with you in the temple...taught you on the mountain....shared in your journey; and as we walked together, I saw light return to blind eyes and healing to broken bodies and spirits. I fed your hungers, hugged your children...
and you trusted me...
walked with me...
believed in me....

My people, what have I done to you?
How have I failed you?

Sylvia Dains

What more could I have done for you that I have not done; and how could you have misunderstood so completely my love for you?

I washed Judas' feet....
trusted him with the purse....
went fishing with Simon and Andrew.
When I called James and John to follow me,
they came immediately -- no looking back.
We were friends....and more....
we were brothers...inseparable.

Wherever we went crowds gathered, eager for stories of the kingdom of heaven --
stories about you, Father; because they knew and believed that whoever had seen me had seen you.

My people, what have I done to you?
How have I grieved you? burdened you?

I offered myself as bread to give you life, and some of you turned away.
Was it fear?

I challenged the scribes and Pharisees,
the keepers of the law.
Although I came to perfect the Law and fulfill
the prophecies, they were blind,
demanding signs; and in their blindness they
built traps made of my words
-- your words, Father.

They seemed always to be looking for reasons to convict me. When I drove the money-changers out of the temple, I gave them just what they were looking for; from there it was only a matter of time. They appealed to Judas' greed, and the price agreed upon was the wage of a rejected shepherd.

My people, what have I done to you?
What more could I have done?

Only a few days ago, you welcomed me as one who comes in the name of the Lord. Yet, today I am here, looking down at what is left of that triumph. I saw the crowd that welcomed me become an angry mob -- a mob that shouted "Crucify!"

The kiss of Judas still on my face,
I stood before Pilate as he washed his hands...
heard Peter's angry voice:
"I do not know the man!"
I saw the light go out of Peter's eyes as mine
met his and a rooster crowed.
I endured as they beat me...
kept silent as they mocked me...
watched as they rolled dice for my clothing.

I have done everything, Father—
everything you asked of me.
I have loved those you sent me,
even those who have run away.
I have planted your Word,
your kingdom, in their hearts...
just as you entrusted it to me.
And now, the work you gave me to do
is finished.
I have been sent by you,
and now return to you.
The rest is up to them.

As the weight of death settles on me, I can
feel it stifling even more my ability to draw a

breath. I can't fight it; I can only know that it's happening, and yield.

My people:
This is my body, given for you...
freely...without condition.
No one takes my life--
it is I who lay it down
--for you....
my gift:
all that I have
all that I am--
so that you may have life
and have it complete.
Mission accomplished, Father.

It is finished.

My people,
do you realize what I have done for you --?
what I have given you?

7

Surrender

Father, it is time. As the day has continued its course, the sky has darkened. There is a sharp chill in the air, and I am so cold. It's been a very long time, and the unrelenting pain has given way to a sort of numbness in my whole body. There is a ringing in my ears; my eyes are swollen almost shut. Whatever I am able to see is not clearly focused. Slowly I feel my body yielding as life slips away.

Father, all of my life has been gift to you. I have heard your voice and followed your way; I have done my best. Many have become followers, but I am grieving the ones who have not - those still lost and searching, afraid in their darkness and blindness. I have wept over Jerusalem, longed to hold her as a mother yearns for her child; but she would not take my hand.

So many times I have gone off alone to be with you, Father; and you have comforted me and sent me back to try again. I had so hoped that the harvest would be more plentiful; but I plead for your mercy and compassion. Many have met you because of me, Father, and many have met me because of you. I know that this is a beginning. I pray that they will proclaim fearlessly the good news of your love -- that they will become instruments of that love, which refuses no one.

I am so cold, Father -- so weak and completely drained. I know that my hour is close, and I am eager to close my eyes and fall into your embrace. Let these last moments glorify you as I pray my life here has done. Let your mercy wrap all of those who have brought me here, and let your forgiveness heal their hearts. Let Peter know that he is forgiven, and give him the boldness to speak the truth you have placed within him.

Father, thank you for allowing me to experience as a man the beauty of your creation, the grace of the humanity you have fashioned. Yes, Father, even though I have experienced humanity at its worst, I have also seen the heights it can reach with you in its heart.

I am at the end of my strength. All of the life you have given me, Father, is pouring itself out -- emptying itself before you -- into you. I offer to you all of myself: body, blood, soul, humanity, divinity -- all those aspects of myself where you have lived and acted. Are you pleased with me today, Father? I offer back to you as my final gift the life you gave me; after all, it was never really mine.

> **Abba -- into your loving hands**
> **I surrender my spirit.**

....and from the heavens, the Father speaks:

**This is my beloved son,
in whom I am well pleased.**

About the Author

Sylvia Dains is a student, a teacher, a speaker, a group facilitator, and a spiritual companion.

The study of Catholic social teaching in light of the Beatitudes awakened a new perspective regarding what God is saying to us today about our call to reflect the teachings of Jesus in our everyday living.

Having spent thirty years as a liturgist and leader of worship, she became a dresser of worship spaces and a crafter of banners and liturgical vestments, so that the setting in which the Word was presented became part of the message. Her study led her to seek ways to present traditional sacred practice in contemporary language and context, to offer the people of God an opportunity to experience and understand in new, hopefully deeper ways. This work is a result of that effort.

Acknowledgements

Nothing of value comes to fruition without the help of many: it's said that "It takes a Village..." This is true regardless of the size or importance of the project; so as I complete this work, I have many to remember and to thank.

My first thanks go to God, who gave me the words, the restlessness to share them, the stubbornness to keep trying, and the friends who never stopped asking "When??"

...to Sister Mary Sylvester, SSJ, my senior English teacher, who encouraged my first attempts at writing and challenged me to more...

...to Sister Mary Robert Thompson, SSMN, my first teacher of Scripture, who became a mentor and friend as I accompanied my husband through his Diaconate formation. She brought the Word to life with her deep devotion to its spirit, and her sense of humor kept me working at it when my enthusiasm weakened...

...to Barbara Shanahan, co-founder with her late husband, Norman, of the Catholic Biblical Studies Program (Buffalo, NY) who introduced me to the Word as I had never before experienced or appreciated it. It was here that I found the basis and inspiration for years of liturgical planning and practice; and here that I first was inspired to breathe life into ideas...

...to the midwives who shared in the birthing of this work, who generously gave of their time and their suggestions, and whose questions and critique held me accountable: Lesa Dailey, Diane Florez, Jean Gladzizewski, and Betty Vernon

...to Maureen ("Mo") Flaherty, who spent hours in the early days reviewing, advising, and encouraging...

...to Christie, who started me on the long process to the "how to's" of publication...

...to Rev. Patrick Zengierski, who refused to allow any further procrastination and who pushed, as only a friend can, to bring the mountain to Mohammed....

...to Rev. Richard Zajac, for his generosity in taking the time to read the work and offer encouragement and written commentary...

...to Rev. James Daprile, for his willingness to review the work, and his kindness in gently offering constructive input...

...to countless friends, who believed, challenged, asked the right questions, encouraged, and hounded...

...finally, to Faye Luckett, whose challenge and support throughout the final editing process held my feet to the fire and kept me working until the day we both knew it was finished...

...Last but never least, to Ron, my own best supporting player and my "word of God" made flesh...

For all of these, and to all of these, I offer humble thanks.

Sylvia Dains

www.ingramcontent.com/pod-product-compliance
Lightning Source LLC
Chambersburg PA
CBHW052208110526
44591CB00012B/2135